5 Steps To
Change Your Beliefs

Inspired Freedom LTD
Kemp House
160 City Road
London EC1V 2NX
United Kingdom
www.inspiredfreedom.ltd

Welcome To

The 5 Step Process

This workbook will give you the structure and tools to powerfully transform your mindset and attract your ultimate dreams.

Do not be fooled how simple the process may seem. Although it will require effort, it is very powerful and can change your life.

The process consists of 5 parts:

1) Become aware of your limiting beliefs
2) Break and dissolve each limiting belief
3) Create new empowering beliefs
4) Build up and strengthen each new empowering belief
5) Condition and integrate your new reality

Make sure you follow each step exactly and completely to get the maximum benefit and end results.

Once you complete this workbook, you can order a new one to work on another area of your life that you wish to transform.

Become Aware of
Your Limiting Beliefs

The first step to changing anything is awareness. To discover the hidden beliefs within your subconscious mind, the following questions will guide you to bringing them to conscious awareness.

Answer the questions without hesitation or filtering out any answers. There is no right or wrong answers here, so it's important to write down whatever thoughts immediately come to your mind.

What did my mother and father say about when I was very young or growing up?

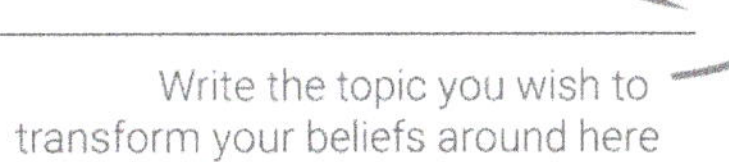

What did my grandmother and grandfather say about ______________________________when I was very young or growing up?

Write your belief topic here

What did my school teachers & friends say about ______________________________ when I was very young or growing up?

Write your belief topic here

When it comes to ______________________ the worst that can happen is...

Write your belief topic here

The worst about ______________________ is...

Write your belief topic here

I feel afraid of ______________________________ because...

Write your belief topic here

I feel overwhelmed with/by ______________________ because...

Write your belief topic here

I feel guilty about ______________________ because...

Write your belief topic here

I feel sad about ______________________ because...

Write your belief topic here

I feel angry about ______________________________ because...

Write your belief topic here

I feel lonely about ______________________ because...

Write your belief topic here

I feel frustrated about ______________________ because...

Write your belief topic here

If I ______________________________, my friends & family will...

Write your ultimate goal, relative to your belief topic

Break & Dissolve
Each Limiting Belief

Every one of the answers you wrote down in the previous questions is a belief, or a thought - that at some level feels true to you, which has been and is subconsciously controlling your thoughts, emotions, decisions and behaviours in this or other areas of your life.

These beliefs have served you at some level up until now, where you'll consciously realize and decide that they no longer have power over you.

In this step of the process, you will start to break each of these limiting beliefs by injecting doubt into them so that they start to crumble and dissolve, making space for new, empowering beliefs to take their place.

In the following pages, for each belief you wrote down, write down at least 23 reasons why that limiting belief is untrue or false.

For example:

If one of my answers was "My friends would become jealous of me if I have a lot of money", then you could write something like:

True friends don't become jealous, it's time I find more genuine friends. My friends only are jealous because they don't believe they too can have a lot of money and be abundant.

The Limiting Belief:

---

23 reasons why this belief is untrue or false:

1)

2)

3)

4)

5)

6)

7)

8)

9)

10)

11)

12)

13)

14)

15)

16)

17)

18)

19)

20)

21)

22)

23)

The Limiting Belief:

---

23 reasons why this belief is untrue or false:

1)

2)

3)

4)

5)

6)

7)

8)

9)

10)

11)

12)

13)

14)

15)

16)

17)

18)

19)

20)

21)

22)

23)

The Limiting Belief:

---

23 reasons why this belief is untrue or false:

1)

2)

3)

4)

5)

6)

7)

8)

9)

10)

11)

12)

13)

14)

15)

16)

17)

18)

19)

20)

21)

22)

23)

The Limiting Belief:

---

23 reasons why this belief is untrue or false:

1)

2)

3)

4)

5)

6)

7)

8)

9)

10)

11)

12)

13)

14)

15)

16)

17)

18)

19)

20)

21)

22)

23)

The Limiting Belief:

---

23 reasons why this belief is untrue or false:

1)

2)

3)

4)

5)

6)

7)

8)

9)

10)

11)

12)

13)

14)

15)

16)

17)

18)

19)

20)

21)

22)

23)

The Limiting Belief:

---

23 reasons why this belief is untrue or false:

1)

2)

3)

4)

5)

6)

7)

8)

9)

10)

11)

12)

13)

14)

15)

16)

17)

18)

19)

20)

21)

22)

23)

The Limiting Belief:

---

23 reasons why this belief is untrue or false:

1)

2)

3)

4)

5)

6)

7)

8)

9)

10)

11)

12)

13)

14)

15)

16)

17)

18)

19)

20)

21)

22)

23)

The Limiting Belief:

____

23 reasons why this belief is untrue or false:

1)

2)

3)

4)

5)

6)

7)

8)

9)

10)

11)

12)

13)

14)

15)

16)

17)

18)

19)

20)

21)

22)

23)

The Limiting Belief:

---

23 reasons why this belief is untrue or false:

1)

2)

3)

4)

5)

6)

7)

8)

9)

10)

11)

12)

13)

14)

15)

16)

17)

18)

19)

20)

21)

22)

23)

The Limiting Belief:

____

23 reasons why this belief is untrue or false:

1)

2)

3)

4)

5)

6)

7)

8)

9)

10)

11)

12)

13)

14)

15)

16)

17)

18)

19)

20)

21)

22)

23)

The Limiting Belief:

---

23 reasons why this belief is untrue or false:

1)

2)

3)

4)

5)

6)

7)

8)

9)

10)

11)

12)

13)

14)

15)

16)

17)

18)

19)

20)

21)

22)

23)

The Limiting Belief:

---

23 reasons why this belief is untrue or false:

1)

2)

3)

4)

5)

6)

7)

8)

9)

10)

11)

12)

13)

14)

15)

16)

17)

18)

19)

20)

21)

22)

23)

The Limiting Belief:

---

23 reasons why this belief is untrue or false:

1)

2)

3)

4)

5)

6)

7)

8)

9)

10)

11)

12)

13)

14)

15)

16)

17)

18)

19)

20)

21)

22)

23)

The Limiting Belief:

---

23 reasons why this belief is untrue or false:

1)

2)

3)

4)

5)

6)

7)

8)

9)

10)

11)

12)

13)

14)

15)

16)

17)

18)

19)

20)

21)

22)

23)

The Limiting Belief:

---

23 reasons why this belief is untrue or false:

1)

2)

3)

4)

5)

6)

7)

8)

9)

10)

11)

12)

13)

14)

15)

16)

17)

18)

19)

20)

21)

22)

23)

The Limiting Belief:

---

23 reasons why this belief is untrue or false:

1)

2)

3)

4)

5)

6)

7)

8)

9)

10)

11)

12)

13)

14)

15)

16)

17)

18)

19)

20)

21)

22)

23)

The Limiting Belief:

____

23 reasons why this belief is untrue or false:

1)

2)

3)

4)

5)

6)

7)

8)

9)

10)

11)

12)

13)

14)

15)

16)

17)

18)

19)

20)

21)

22)

23)

The Limiting Belief:

---

23 reasons why this belief is untrue or false:

1)

2)

3)

4)

5)

6)

7)

8)

9)

10)

11)

12)

13)

14)

15)

16)

17)

18)

19)

20)

21)

22)

23)

The Limiting Belief:

---

23 reasons why this belief is untrue or false:

1)

2)

3)

4)

5)

6)

7)

8)

9)

10)

11)

12)

13)

14)

15)

16)

17)

18)

19)

20)

21)

22)

23)

The Limiting Belief:

---

23 reasons why this belief is untrue or false:

1)

2)

3)

4)

5)

6)

7)

8)

9)

10)

11)

12)

13)

14)

15)

16)

17)

18)

19)

20)

21)

22)

23)

The Limiting Belief:

---

23 reasons why this belief is untrue or false:

1)

2)

3)

4)

5)

6)

7)

8)

9)

10)

11)

12)

13)

14)

15)

16)

17)

18)

19)

20)

21)

22)

23)

The Limiting Belief:

---

23 reasons why this belief is untrue or false:

1)

2)

3)

4)

5)

6)

7)

8)

9)

10)

11)

12)

13)

14)

15)

16)

17)

18)

19)

20)

21)

22)

23)

The Limiting Belief:

---

23 reasons why this belief is untrue or false:

1)

2)

3)

4)

5)

6)

7)

8)

9)

10)

11)

12)

13)

14)

15)

16)

17)

18)

19)

20)

21)

22)

23)

The Limiting Belief:

---

23 reasons why this belief is untrue or false:

1)

2)

3)

4)

5)

6)

7)

8)

9)

10)

11)

12)

13)

14)

15)

16)

17)

18)

19)

20)

21)

22)

23)

The Limiting Belief:

---

23 reasons why this belief is untrue or false:

1)

2)

3)

4)

5)

6)

7)

8)

9)

10)

11)

12)

13)

14)

15)

16)

17)

18)

19)

20)

21)

22)

23)

Create New
Empowering Beliefs

Congratulations! I know it wasn't easy, but you did it - that's what counts. If you haven't yet, it's important you complete this part fully before you move onto this step. The old, limiting beliefs should feel like they don't hold truth anymore.

The next step is to replace each limiting belief with a new, empowering belief. For each of the limiting beliefs you dissolved in step 2, write down the opposite or more empowering version of that statement.

For example:

If you had a limiting belief of "starting a business is risky", write down something like "starting a business is the most secure thing I can do for my future and my family"

It's OK if it doesn't sound true... yet! You'll be working on that in step 4.

Your New Empowering Beliefs:

1)

2)

3)

4)

5)

6)

7)

8)

9)

10)

11)

12)

13)

14)

15)

16)

17)

18)

19)

20)

21)

22)

23)

24)

25)

Build Up & Strengthen Each New

Empowering Belief

The next step is similar to step 2 of the process, except that for each new empowering belief that you wrote down, you will write 23 reasons why each of your new empowering beliefs are TRUE!

Here's an example:

If your new empowering belief was "starting a business is the most secure thing I can do for myself and my family", then you could write:

- A job is only one income stream, which is dependent on my employer, while my own business can have multiple income streams and is dependent on me.

- I own my business, but I can't own a job, which allows me to build wealth long term into the future.

- I am the business decision maker, which puts my destiny in my own hands, rather than into my employer's hands.

- I can have uncapped earning potential in my business as well as tax-saving advantages which allows me to build a more secure financial future than a limited salary in a single job.

The New Empowering Belief:

---

23 reasons why this belief is true:

1)

2)

3)

4)

5)

6)

7)

8)

9)

10)

11)

12)

13)

14)

15)

16)

17)

18)

19)

20)

21)

22)

23)

The New Empowering Belief:

---

23 reasons why this belief is true:

1)

2)

3)

4)

5)

6)

7)

8)

9)

10)

11)

12)

13)

14)

15)

16)

17)

18)

19)

20)

21)

22)

23)

The New Empowering Belief:

---

23 reasons why this belief is true:

1)

2)

3)

4)

5)

6)

7)

8)

9)

10)

11)

12)

13)

14)

15)

16)

17)

18)

19)

20)

21)

22)

23)

The New Empowering Belief:

---

23 reasons why this belief is true:

1)

2)

3)

4)

5)

6)

7)

8)

9)

10)

11)

12)

13)

14)

15)

16)

17)

18)

19)

20)

21)

22)

23)

The New Empowering Belief:

---

23 reasons why this belief is true:

1)

2)

3)

4)

5)

6)

7)

8)

9)

10)

11)

12)

13)

14)

15)

16)

17)

18)

19)

20)

21)

22)

23)

The New Empowering Belief:

---

23 reasons why this belief is true:

1)

2)

3)

4)

5)

6)

7)

8)

9)

10)

11)

12)

13)

14)

15)

16)

17)

18)

19)

20)

21)

22)

23)

The New Empowering Belief:

---

23 reasons why this belief is true:

1)

2)

3)

4)

5)

6)

7)

8)

9)

10)

11)

12)

13)

14)

15)

16)

17)

18)

19)

20)

21)

22)

23)

The New Empowering Belief:

---

23 reasons why this belief is true:

1)

2)

3)

4)

5)

6)

7)

8)

9)

10)

11)

12)

13)

14)

15)

16)

17)

18)

19)

20)

21)

22)

23)

The New Empowering Belief:

---

23 reasons why this belief is true:

1)

2)

3)

4)

5)

6)

7)

8)

9)

10)

11)

12)

13)

14)

15)

16)

17)

18)

19)

20)

21)

22)

23)

The New Empowering Belief:

---

23 reasons why this belief is true:

1)

2)

3)

4)

5)

6)

7)

8)

9)

10)

11)

12)

13)

14)

15)

16)

17)

18)

19)

20)

21)

22)

23)

The New Empowering Belief:

---

23 reasons why this belief is true:

1)

2)

3)

4)

5)

6)

7)

8)

9)

10)

11)

12)

13)

14)

15)

16)

17)

18)

19)

20)

21)

22)

23)

The New Empowering Belief:

---

23 reasons why this belief is true:

1)

2)

3)

4)

5)

6)

7)

8)

9)

10)

11)

12)

13)

14)

15)

16)

17)

18)

19)

20)

21)

22)

23)

The New Empowering Belief:

---

23 reasons why this belief is true:

1)

2)

3)

4)

5)

6)

7)

8)

9)

10)

11)

12)

13)

14)

15)

16)

17)

18)

19)

20)

21)

22)

23)

The New Empowering Belief:

---

23 reasons why this belief is true:

1)

2)

3)

4)

5)

6)

7)

8)

9)

10)

11)

12)

13)

14)

15)

16)

17)

18)

19)

20)

21)

22)

23)

The New Empowering Belief:

---

23 reasons why this belief is true:

1)

2)

3)

4)

5)

6)

7)

8)

9)

10)

11)

12)

13)

14)

15)

16)

17)

18)

19)

20)

21)

22)

23)

The New Empowering Belief:

---

23 reasons why this belief is true:

1)

2)

3)

4)

5)

6)

7)

8)

9)

10)

11)

12)

13)

14)

15)

16)

17)

18)

19)

20)

21)

22)

23)

The New Empowering Belief:

---

23 reasons why this belief is true:

1)

2)

3)

4)

5)

6)

7)

8)

9)

10)

11)

12)

13)

14)

15)

16)

17)

18)

19)

20)

21)

22)

23)

The New Empowering Belief:

---

23 reasons why this belief is true:

1)

2)

3)

4)

5)

6)

7)

8)

9)

10)

11)

12)

13)

14)

15)

16)

17)

18)

19)

20)

21)

22)

23)

The New Empowering Belief:

---

23 reasons why this belief is true:

1)

2)

3)

4)

5)

6)

7)

8)

9)

10)

11)

12)

13)

14)

15)

16)

17)

18)

19)

20)

21)

22)

23)

The New Empowering Belief:

---

23 reasons why this belief is true:

1)

2)

3)

4)

5)

6)

7)

8)

9)

10)

11)

12)

13)

14)

15)

16)

17)

18)

19)

20)

21)

22)

23)

The New Empowering Belief:

---

23 reasons why this belief is true:

1)

2)

3)

4)

5)

6)

7)

8)

9)

10)

11)

12)

13)

14)

15)

16)

17)

18)

19)

20)

21)

22)

23)

The New Empowering Belief:

---

23 reasons why this belief is true:

1)

2)

3)

4)

5)

6)

7)

8)

9)

10)

11)

12)

13)

14)

15)

16)

17)

18)

19)

20)

21)

22)

23)

The New Empowering Belief:

---

23 reasons why this belief is true:

1)

2)

3)

4)

5)

6)

7)

8)

9)

10)

11)

12)

13)

14)

15)

16)

17)

18)

19)

20)

21)

22)

23)

The New Empowering Belief:

---

23 reasons why this belief is true:

1)

2)

3)

4)

5)

6)

7)

8)

9)

10)

11)

12)

13)

14)

15)

16)

17)

18)

19)

20)

21)

22)

23)

The New Empowering Belief:

---

23 reasons why this belief is true:

1)

2)

3)

4)

5)

6)

7)

8)

9)

10)

11)

12)

13)

14)

15)

16)

17)

18)

19)

20)

21)

22)

23)

Condition & Integrate
Your New Reality

Like fragile seedlings, your new empowering beliefs will need to be carefully nurtured and "watered" with daily focus & concentration until they are fully conditioned and integrated in your subconscious mind.

This process will effectively establish & grow new unconscious thought patterns & neural pathways that will cement your empowering beliefs in your brain.

These new beliefs, once they have become part of you, will influence your emotions and behaviour in new ways, resulting in new actions and outcomes in your life.

There are many methods in which you can condition & integrate your new empowering beliefs, but we will highlight our favourite, for you to practice.

Discover the Power of
Afformations®

Noah St. John is the creator of Afformations®, a method that is more powerful than traditional affirmations because it bypasses your analytical mind's gatekeeper which says "Yeah, right!" when you affirm or say an affirmation like "I am rich".

Instead, this simple method turns the affirmation into a question, such as: "Why is it so easy for me to be rich?".

This activates your brain's natural tendency to continually search for answers to questions, which focuses it on what you want, rather than what you don't want.

You'll be able to avoid the feelings of doubt & resistance when you first start saying these new statements, so you can easily integrate them.

Putting this into practice, try rephrasing all of your new empowering beliefs in the form of:

"Why is it so easy for me to ______________________________________"
and fill in the blank with the new belief you want to condition your subconscious mind with.

Try This:

To feel the difference between before and after, first say your statement without the question phrase in front of it.

Notice and be aware if you feel resistance while saying it or if your body tenses up or you feel any other signs that indicate you don't quite believe it yet completely, 100%.

Next, say the same statement but with the question phrase in front of it, "Why is it so easy for me to...". Notice your body and be aware of how much easier it is to say it without feeling resistance or hesitation that may have been there before.

Daily Exercise:

Choose a maximum of three statements (new empowering beliefs), and over a 14 day period, repeat them in the question form out loud at least 50 times, two to three times per day.

First thing in the morning when you wake up, and evening before you go to bed are the most effective times because your brain waves slow down and your subconscious mind is more receptive to suggestions.

After 14 days, or whenever you intuitively feel that you've fully integrated this set of empowering beliefs and they feel true to you when you say them out loud, choose the next three to integrate and repeat the process.

Empowering Belief Set #1:

1)

2)

3)

Empowering Belief Set #2:

1)

2)

3)

Empowering Belief Set #3:

1)

2)

3)

Empowering Belief Set #4:

1)

2)

3)

Empowering Belief Set #5:

1)

2)

3)

Empowering Belief Set #6:

1)

2)

3)

Empowering Belief Set #7:

1)

2)

3)

Empowering Belief Set #8:

1)

2)

3)

Empowering Belief Set #9:

1)

2)

3)

Create Your Own Unique
Affirmation Tracks

At Mindset Magnetics,® we developed a tool called My Affirmation Tracks which allows you to quickly and easily create your very own unique audio affirmation tracks to listen to daily and reinforce positive thought patterns and beliefs.

These tracks are a combination of professionally recorded affirmation statements which you can select from a range of topics, designed to empower & focus your mind on exactly what you want to create & attract in your life.

It only takes a few minutes and we are expanding the database daily. If you can't find certain statements that you want us to add, or have suggestions for improvements, we would love to hear from you so we can add these into our future releases.

Get started now, with a special 50% voucher code as a thanks for taking action and transforming your mindset.

Visit MyAffirmationTracks.com and enter this code on checkout:

MMCYB50

What's Next?

We hope you continue to use this process to transform your beliefs and mindset so you can overcome blocks and achieve everything you desire in your life. Remember, the more energy and effort you put into this process, the more rewarding and effective your results will be over time.

Keep consistent, and if you need additional support, head on over to **mindsetmagnetics.com** to book a 1-on-1 coaching call to get guidance on your specific mindset challenges.

www.ingramcontent.com/pod-product-compliance
Ingram Content Group UK Ltd.
Pitfield, Milton Keynes, MK11 3LW, UK
UKHW061949290726
14090UKWH00021B/1142

9 781919 629704